My English Cow

A Young Man's Poetic Musings

Tom Birk

Artwork and poetry
created by
a young man
long before he even
thought of becoming
Dr. Tom Birk.

ISBN:978-0-9847111-8-5 Copyright © 2017 Tom Birk,D.O.

Library of Congress Control Number: 2017901915
Published by **Olive Press Publisher**, Lowville, NY

OlivePressPublisher.com

To people young and old
and their
innocent,
silly thoughts.

TABLE OF CONTENTS

Dear Owner,

    I like my new home

    my new life too

    I'll eat and sleep

    is what I'll do

    I'll warn you of strangers

    but first I'll grow teeth

    And I'll gnaw on the furniture

    or whatever's beneath

    I'll pee on the carpet

    then be scolded when found

    But you'll learn to love me

    your unpapertrained hound

                Sincerely,

                The Pup

Sarah Sally Sow

(RHYMES WITH "COW")

Sarah Sally Sow

a most depressing cow

never smiles or laughs or ever says hello

Her milk is always lumpy

'cause she is always grumpy

she frowns and mopes and always moves so slow

So if your milk is sour

it was because the hour

the farmer milked a most depress-ed cow

It's never marked on bottles

but I bet it's from the throttles

of the sad and low down Sarah Sally Sow

LAND OF CABBAGE

In the land of cabbage

lives a dream I know

I once was a rabbit

in a picture show

and in this land of cabbage

or so my part did go

I ate all I wanted

and I love cabbage—ya know?

OLD TOASTER

One second two second

three seconds four

One minute and a half

just wait a little more

Do you smell something burning?

The toast I think is cooked

POP—oh darn it burned again

I knew I should've looked

CRAZY WORLD

I grew up on an english farm

with english cows who drank

english tea and ate

green grass

Wore an english

uniform and said english prayers

and studied, ... French

Crazy World it is

SPECIAL RECIPE

Goat cheese is nice

to have on rice

with grape jam and lime twister

chili sauce ketchup

and just a touch of salt

and then feed it to my sister

Haircut Like Dad Wants It

Today I get a haircut
my father drives me there
He wants the barber Charlie
to cut off most my hair
To comb it over with the gell
that sloppy V.O.-5
And look just like my Dad does
an old man not alive

Come on Dad, I look good now!
How 'bout just a trim?
As the trim turns into baldness
I'm getting very grim
And as the barber's speaking
with Dad and all the while
They've both condemned this kid a month
to hair that's out of style

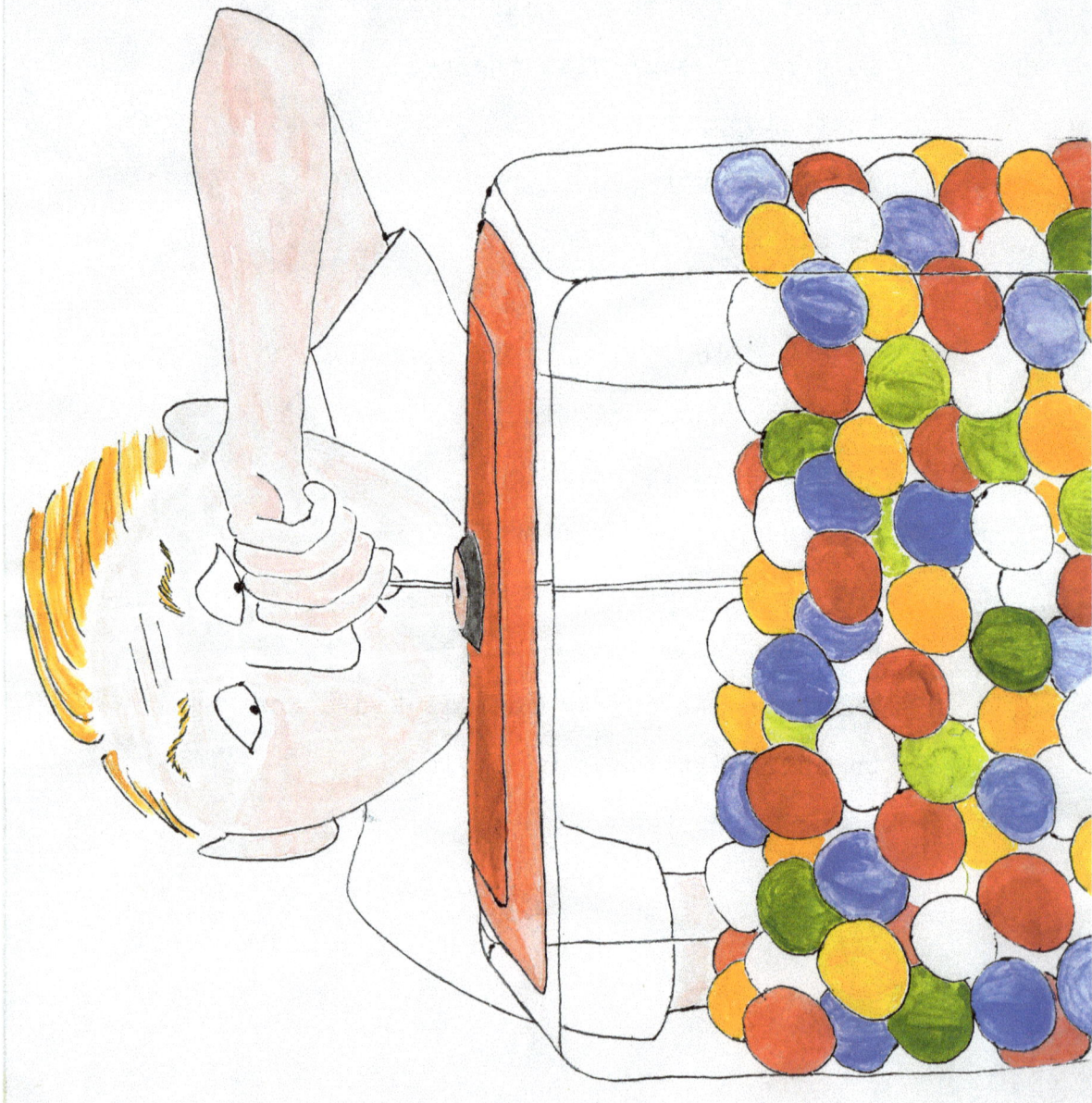

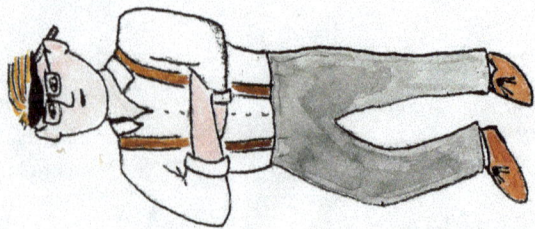

GUMBALL MACHINE

Gumball machine

give me a green

I'll give you a slug—don't be fickle

If the manager watches

I'll take what you give

whilst I give you a nickel

MARTIAN

When I'm by myself

I can belch and start afartin

Pick my nose and spit

drink milk straight from the carton

Wipe my mouth on my sleeve

and sneak some candy bars

Dad tells me that I came from Mom

Mom says I came from Mars

Pop Pop and Nan Nan's House

Come to the Sunday
Afternoon I know
to the Pop Pop love you couch
and the Nan Nan show
Nan Nan in the kitchen
she baked a cake for me
Talking to my mother
they share a cup of tea
Pop Pop watching baseball
thinks us kids as neat
rolls his cigarette
he offers us a treat
But don't spoil your dinner
your father won't approve
Yes—you know your father
antagonistic scrooge
But who cares anyhow
as Nan Nan plays away
music on piano
from a different day
The roast is cooking steadfast
fresh cole slaw's in the fridge
with homemade mashed potatoes
is my brother's favorite dish
And we're thinking of our homelife
where we can play some ball
what can we do for fun here
if anything at all
But now that I'm maturer now
(if anyone can see)
I'm glad I had those visits
to my only family.
I love them so.

JUNK DRAWER

itsgot my baseball cards and wallet
my pins my gum my pens
itsgot my jokebook and the camera
which needs film again
itsgot my spoon with pooh-bear
abreakfast prize-you know
itsgot the seed I wait to dry
to plant in spring and grow
itsgot my autograph of Garvey
itsgot my magic cards
itsgot my lucky rabbits' foot
and ball of twine in yards
itsgot my Quisp-guy prize inside
who beat that feller Quake
another prize from cereal
that I'll never use or break
itsgot my comics, hundreds all
I mail to get a prize
for which my parents discredit
and always criticize
itsgot my flashlight chain below
on top of the baseball poster
itsgot some dirt (and a few crumbs)
from a Pop Tart from the toaster
itsgot my compass in the back
pointing towards northwest
my handwarmer is next to that
for which I love the best
These are just a few things
in a box all full of pleasure
Mom calls it the "Junk Drawer"
but really it's my treasure

FREQUENT LIAR

Did I tell you 'bout the day

your mother bit a dog?

It was quite a misty day

and the air was full of fog

It happened on a Saturday

just after the fire

and if you hadn't guessed by now

I'm quite a frequent liar

SOMETHING'S DRIPPING DOWN ON THE REFRIGERATOR FLOOR

Something's dripping down on the refrigerator floor
Something really goopy that we don't want anymore
Something super sticky we no longer want to store
and I know just what it is.
It could be from the cranberry that's slightly tilted east
or the leftovers from Thurseday (We had slightly sloppy beast)
or the juices from the coffee grinds (Mom likes to use em twice)
but I know what it really is-it really isn't nice
The bottom shelf is gooey now and it's starting now to toughen
Soon we'll have bananas glued and also Monday's stuffing
Fresh carrots with the cucumbers mixed with tonights tomatoes
All stuck together mushed in gooey mashed potatoes
Oh WHAT has CAUSED this sloppy mess
this dripping fluid fizz
You can guess all you want
but I know what it is
I'll never tell who did it
would have happened anyhow.
AND I THINK SOMEONE SHOULD CLEAN THIS MESS!
Okay Mom, I'll clean it now.

DEAR CHILDREN

Dear children listen closely

to what I have to say

All in this world is not pretty

happy or gay

And some bad things do happen

that make us angry and mad

Sometimes we feel so closed in

awe struck and sad

It's then that time that we must think

of great things we can do

Then it's all the sweeter when we reach

all our dreams come true

Not only are we thinking good

and feeling so much lighter

But a smile is like the sun you know

it makes the world much brighter

RONALD BRADLEY'S HOUSE

Monopoly at Ronald Bradley's
he used to serve us lots of snackees
His parents never ever home
so we'd pig out, us kids alone
We'd watch T.V. and play, you see
play "All Day Monopoly"
All my brothers-yes they'd play
to have some fun for that day
But at dinnertime we'd eat no more
because we were full to the core
with Hershey Bars and sweets galore
from Ronald Bradley's house

The Joy of a Friend

The joy of a friend is such that
the joy of a friend it is
When somebody anybody does that
while sharing that hers and his
When something's the matter with nothing
never the feeling so strong
'cause when a friend comes to share
the courage does 'Dare'
and helps us to get along

FRED THE FRYING FISH

I'm Fred the frying fish
'cause I'd make quite a dish
Catching me would make that young boy grateful
But no matter how he's trying
He can't get me frying
or baked or broiled to be somebody's plateful
And so he'll look and look
Disguise his dangling hook
He knows I'd make somebody's dish a winner
But I guess until that day
I'll just swim away
Thinking of that lad just getting thinner
He'll just have to eat something else for dinner.

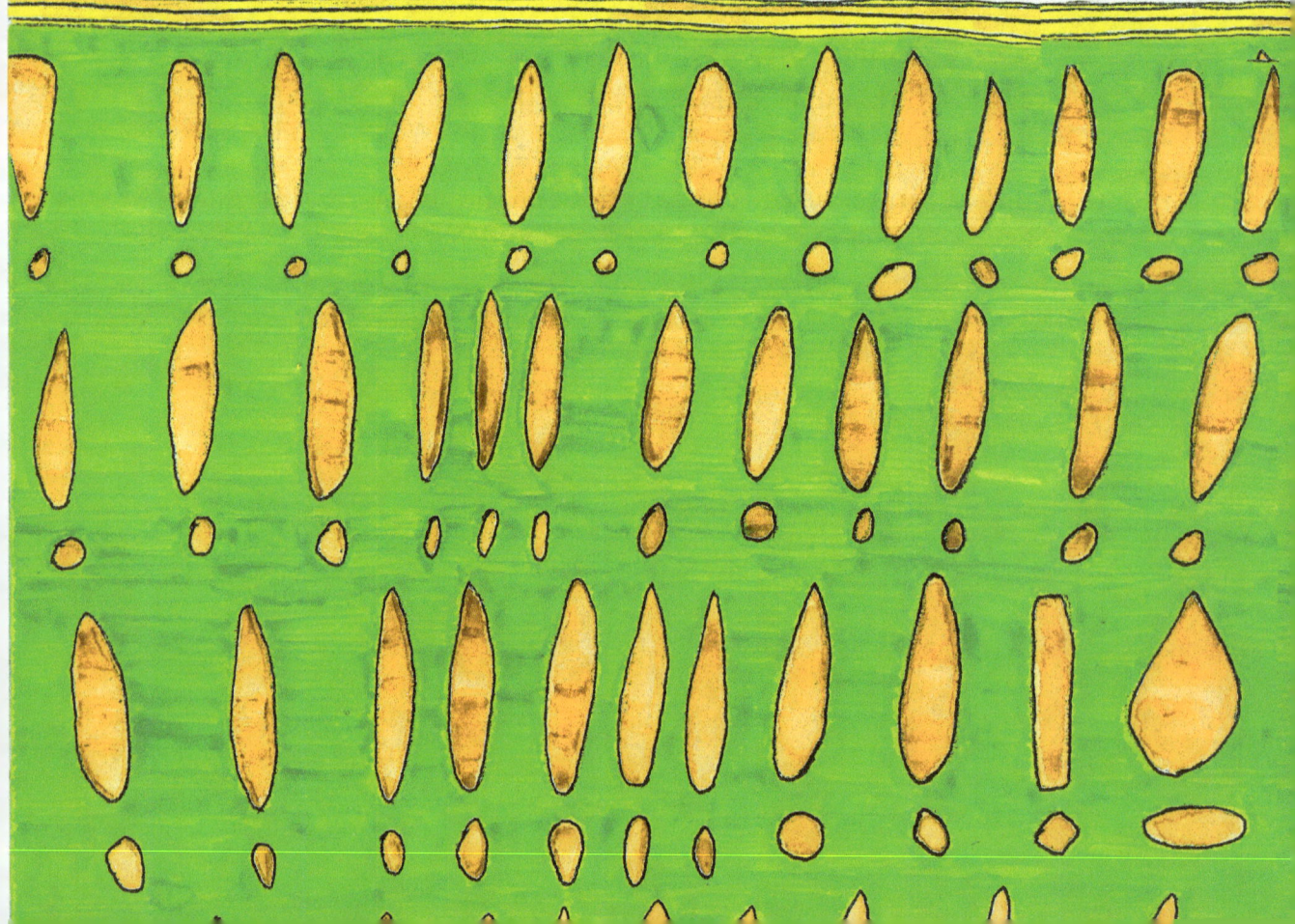

IF

If life were that simple
we'd all live in homes
there'd be clothes on our skins
and meats for our bones
if life were that simple
we could all be understood
and the unity of love
would be a shared brotherhood
if life were that simple
these means we would do
to take the chance to make
all our dreams come true
See the world as it is
it won't come easily
but life is that simple child
and all of these can be

ONE OF GOD'S I AM

I have a cloud in my pocket

in case I want to dream

I wear prescription glasses

to see just what they mean

I also carry keys

to unlock many doors

and also keys to lock them

in case I want no more

I walk on my soul

so I always know the path

and I learned how to count

all the blessings that I have

I comb stars in my hair

'cause I'm so beautiful

I never wear a watch

my time is never dull

I have a spring in my step

to flow with rhythm and

a scale is on my head

to judge and understand

All these things are mine

'cause I am just a man

But in God's light I shine

'cause one of God's I am

ST. GEORGIO

St. Georgio

was he a saint?

Or is he the face

on a can of paint?

He sounds more like

spagghetti sauce

St. Georgio?

I'm at a loss

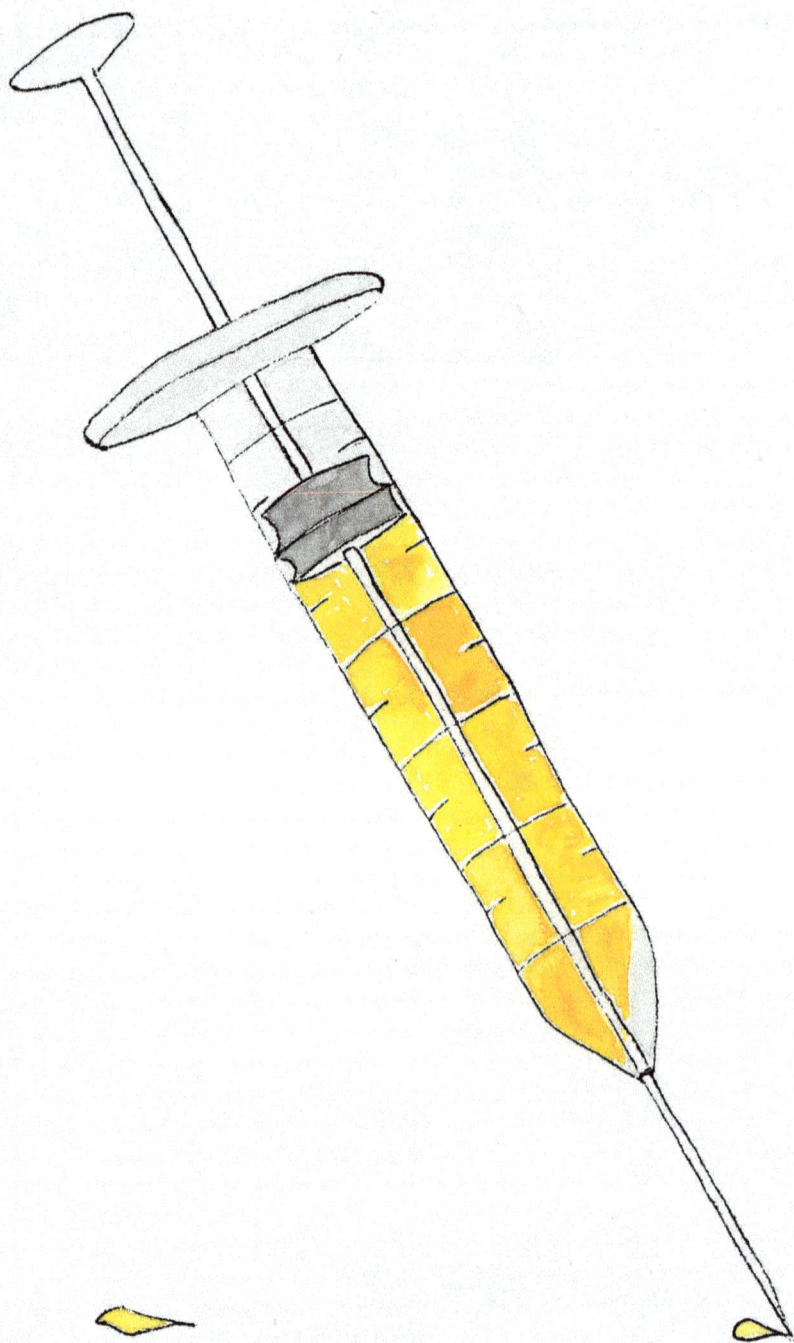

ALLERGY SHOT

Go to the doctor

like a freak

for a stupid shot

once a week

So I'm not allergic

to grass and trees

So I don't get asthma

and start to wheez

but Geez

it don't work anyhow

TOM SAYS GOODNIGHT

To a better morrow
with joyous fun
To every daughter
every son
To a sunny day
with a comfortable breeze
May you never be allergic
and have to sneeze

Goodnight Children

and God bless you

www.ingramcontent.com/pod-product-compliance
Lightning Source LLC
Chambersburg PA
CBHW050659110426
42739CB00035B/3459